A TASTE OF HUNGARY

45 év hosszú idő...
de jó volt újra találkozni.
A JOBST családnak sok
szeretettel: Hemző Károly
1994. ápr. 3.

THE
HORTOBÁGY REGION

Text by
ZOLTÁN HALÁSZ

Photographs by
KÁROLY HEMZŐ

CORVINA

THE HORTOBÁGY REGION

DEBRECEN AND THE HORTOBÁGY

THE eastern part of the Hungarian Alföld (the Great Plain) is popularly associated with the concept of the *puszta,* that is to say a flat, treeless area, covered with scant grass. In actual fact, however, the principal town of the eastern Alföld, Debrecen, together with its surroundings, is more noted for its parks, gardens and stretches of woodland, even though the most extensive of the remaining Alföld *pusztas,* the Hortobágy, is to be found in the vicinity. The streets and public squares of Debrecen itself are a mass of trees and flowers, while the great municipal park, the Nagyerdő, is given over to attractive promenades, amusement places, a boating-lake, and restaurants. During August, the whole of Debrecen has the appearance of a single flower-garden, as the Carnival of Flowers wends its way along the streets and through the squares.

The inhabitants' love of nature certainly has something to do with the history of the town, the citizens of which, although they earned their living principally through commerce and handicrafts, never abandoned farming entirely. The pastures and ploughland surrounding the town were municipal property, and were worked by the citizens on the principle—enshrined in a regulatory ordinance of 1517—that the land area entitlement per household bore a direct relationship to the taxes paid. The main source of prosperity was stock-raising. The long-horned grey Hungarian prime beef cattle were despatched from the area on the hoof, and found a ready market far and wide. The merchants of Debrecen formed themselves into companies, and sent off their wares under safe escort

to Prague, Vienna, Nuremberg, and Cracow: leather goods, cloth, gold and silverware, and the products of the locksmiths, swordsmiths, and other craftsmen.

The income from the sale of livestock and handicrafts and from commerce generally, came in useful among other things, when it was a question of delivering Debrecen from the perils and destruction which threatened it from all quarters. The citizens preferred, on the whole, to open their purses and pay, rather than resort to arms, when some enemy menaced the town, and there were many occasions on which, by the prudent exercise of an eye for the main chance, they were able to save the town during the centuries of storm and strife. It was a decisive moment in Debrecen's history when through the exercise of "citizen-diplomacy", the town was able to ward off the Turkish onslaught at the time of the conquest by the latter of Buda, and the tripartite division of Hungary. While Debrecen tried, through money and diplomacy, to come to terms with the Sultan, and with the Habsburgs who held the northern and western parts of the country, its heart lay more with Transylvania, in whose prosperity the town was also able to share. István Bocskai, Prince of Transylvania, gained freedom of worship for the Protestants under the Treaty of Vienna in 1606, which meant that the inhabitants of Debrecen—who had embraced the Reformed Church—could freely subscribe to their "Helvetic religious sect" (i.e. Calvinism) there-

Coat-of-arms of the town of Debrecen on the façade of the town hall (top). The delicious Country soup is made of three kinds of meat (right)

4

MILD FLAVOURS AT THE GOLDEN BULL

THE centuries-old connection with Transylvania makes its influence felt in the delicate, mildly seasoned dishes to be sampled in Debrecen. I had this experience for the first time in the dining room of the Golden Bull Hotel, where the effect was enhanced by the brilliant, dreamlike colours of the so-called "glass room" built in the Art Nouveau style at the beginning of this century. My dish of stuffed vine leaves might well have come straight from the kitchen, redolent with the scent of fine herbs, of Anna Bornemissza, consort of the Prince of Transylvania. Hence the hint of fresh dill in the stuffed vine leaves, and of marjoram, tarragon, rosemary, and cress in other dishes offered. However, before starting on the stuffed vine leaves, I was served a magnificent soup, which deserves special mention. It goes by the name of "Country soup", and it is said to have originated in a village near Debrecen. Its present delicious, intricately flavoured guise no doubt owes much to the head chef of the Golden Bull, József Nagy, who extended the original basic ingredient—shoulder of pork—to also include beef and chicken. Add to these mushrooms, soup vegetables, onions, pepper and sweet paprika, and the result is a superb combination of flavours. But the best is still to come: once the soup is ready you

after. The Reformed College founded in 1538 became, thanks to the support of the Princes of Transylvania and the congregation of Debrecen, an important centre of scholarship and education in Hungarian life.

This educational foundation became, in the course of time, the spiritual centre not only of Debrecen, but of all Hungarian Protestantism. It maintained active links—and still does—with universities in Switzerland, France, Germany, the Netherlands, Great Britain and the United States. In the vicinity of the College stands another of Debrecen's famous historic buildings, the Great Reformed Church, built in the Neo-Classical style in the 19th century to replace the earlier church which was destroyed during the fire of 1802. The Hungarian parliament met in the Great Church on two occasions: first during the War of Independence against the Habsburgs in 1848, when the two chambers held a joint session to read out Lajos Kossuth's declaration of Hungarian Independence and a decree deposing the Habsburgs from the throne of Hungary. The second occasion was towards the end of the Second World War, during the winter of 1944–45, when the Provisional National Assembly held its sessions in the Great Church.

Debrecen's famous historic building, the Great Reformed Church (top). The Art Nouveau "Glass Room" of the Golden Bull Hotel, built towards the beginning of the century (right)

pour it into an earthenware casserole, seal the top with pastry dough, and put the whole thing into a hot oven to bake. The pastry gradually absorbs the delicious flavours of the soup during the baking process, finally achieving a state of perfect harmony with the contents of the casserole. Of course, both pastry and contents must be eaten together: you use a spoon for the soup, and take bites out of the pastry now and then, both processes forming an essential part of the ritual connected with the consumption of this dish.

By the time I had worked my way through this substantial soup—the pastry as well—I had had just about enough, so I was particularly pleased that the second course consisted only of the aforementioned stuffed vine leaves. According to the original Székely (East Transylvanian Magyar) recipe, which is faithfully followed to this day by the traditionally minded cooks of Debrecen, the filling should be made of veal, pork, onions browned in fat, and rice. This mixture is wrapped in tender vine leaves which are then cooked in water containing bunches of vine shoots. The final touch of flavour is provided by the presence of the normal Hungarian roux (used to thicken sauces) and sour cream, together with an almost imperceptible taste of fresh dill. Also in the tradition of Transylvanian cuisine was the "pastry horn", prepared from feather-light pastry sprinkled with sugar and crushed walnuts. When it emerged that Debrecen's acknowledged expert in the preparation of this delicacy worked at the patisserie just

by the Golden Bull, I decided to pay him a visit after lunch. There I had the opportunity to see him in action, and to marvel at his special skills.

First of all, when the dough had risen, he cut it into pieces each weighing about 300 g (10 oz). Next he rolled them out into thin strips which he wound round a number of previously oiled cylindrical spits in such a manner that their surfaces were completely covered. Then he brushed the dough over with milk, rolled the spits in a mixture of sugar and ground walnuts, and put them into the oven to bake. He told me that, in the old days, they used to bake over the embers of a corn-cob fire, turning the spits whenever it seemed necessary, in order to ensure that the pastry browned evenly. What I saw in Debrecen, however, was far removed from the old traditional method: the pastry-wrapped spits were turned inside the glassed-in oven by means of an electric motor, and all the baker had to do was to take them out when the pastry was nice and brown and the air was filled with a delicious smell. "Even doing it this way I can hardly keep pace," he remarked, by way of excuse for the innovation. "I bake three times a day, and they're all taken up as soon as they're ready."

Debrecen's famous "Carnival of Flowers" takes place every year in August. The so-called "cut-off steeple" of the town's most ancient church can be seen in the background, behind the girls performing the "carafe dance" (top and left)

It seems that pastry horns have come into fashion once more, which is not surprising in view of the pleasant memories conjured up by their sweet nutty flavour—memories of afternoons at the Golden Bull in days gone by, with elegantly dressed ladies seated by their coffees with whipped cream and pastry horns. The Golden Bull itself gives rise to nostalgic recollections of this sort. A palatial edifice in the Art Nouveau style, it was built at the beginning of this century to replace an earlier, 19th-century building, during a period of marked activity and rising prosperity in Debrecen, as is reflected in the profusion of stained glass windows, cupolas, statues and beaten-copper ornamentation. The architect himself was an interesting personality. Alfréd Hajós, the designer of the building, was not only an excellent engineer, he was also an outstanding athlete. There is a show-case in the entrance hall of the hotel which—at the time of my visit—contained medals and cups won by him at various world competitions. Amongst them could be seen the gold medal awarded to him at the 1896 Olympics in Athens, where he won the 100 metres free-style swimming event with a time of 1 minute 22.2 seconds. This made him the first Hungarian modern Olympic champion.

FLAVOURS OF THE HAJDÚSÁG REGION

IT is a characteristic of Debrecen that, as you proceed outwards from the centre, the town gradually acquires a more and more provincial aspect, until eventually you get the feeling that you are in a village. In fact it is a very pleasant contrast from the bustle of the town centre to arrive, after only half an hour's stroll—or 5 minutes by car—in an area where there is nothing but gardens and village-style houses, and where idyllic calm reigns.

The Czinege family live in an area the village atmosphere of which is as yet undisturbed by the forceful intrusion of ferro-concrete structures. A little further into town, however, the streets are lined with single-storey, middle-class houses, reflecting with their Neo-Classical façades and puritan simplicity of line a strict bourgeois morality. The Czineges' cooking arrangements are based on the traditional dishes of the Hajdúság region, as the visitor is immediately aware from the appetizing smells coming from the kitchen. However, I should mention here that the Hajdúság is primarily a historical and geographical concept, which has little if anything to do with gastronomic matters. The name began to be used in the 16th

"Country soup" served in an earthenware casserole sealed with a layer of pastry (bottom left), and the feather-light pastry horn

(bottom right). Not exactly a light meal, but very delicious nevertheless: the roasted pork knuckle, done to a turn (right)

vegetables, mushrooms and other ingredients), which had been removed from the soup when half done and sprinkled with salt, pepper, and a little beer, and put into the oven to roast until golden brown. It was brought to the table garnished with potatoes cooked around it in the same pan and consequently permeated with all the delicious flavours of the roast. The pickled gherkins served as accompaniment also deserve special mention. According to Mrs. Czinege, their flavour and crispness owed much to her use of a pig's bladder to seal the jars before putting the gherkins away, rather than the usual type of sealing material. Of course, it was not possible to obtain such a thing from a shop nowadays. You had to wait for pig-killing time, and then, when you had got the bladder, you had to make sure you cleaned it carefully before putting it away in the larder to dry. When you needed to use it, you had to soak it in water first, then cut it into pieces the right size. In this way the gherkins were not only protected from the outside air, but the porosity of the bladder "allowed them to breathe", as Mrs. Czinege put it.

As we slowly ate our way through the chicken, the conversation turned on the types of food prepared at pig-killing time, since that was when the necessary ingredients were most readily available. Cinnamon flavoured sausages, for example, which were Józsi Czinege's particular speciality. You need several different parts of the animal for these: the lean meat under the belly, a small quantity of lung, perhaps some tongue and liver too. The ingredients must be well cooked first in a tasty meat stock, then allowed to cool before being put through the mincer and finally kneaded together with boiled rice, salt, pepper, paprika and—obviously, in view of the name—with powdered cinnamon. The mixture is then used to stuff the well-washed sausage skins, and the sausages, when fried, are such a favourite with everyone that the Czinege grandchildren, for example, are happy to live off them for a whole week—even when served cold, said Mr. Czinege.

While cinnamon flavoured sausages are a seasonal dish prepared at pig-killing time, tripe done in the Hajdúság way is not tied to any particular time of the year. If any fresh tripe happens to be available, and some smoked pig's head (ears included), then people are glad to make it and serve it at any time. I particularly mention the ears because diced and fried with onions they make a fine, crisp, tasty addition to the dish. In fact, without them, tripe Hajdúság style would not be the genuine thing at all.

First of all the tripe must be prepared by parboiling it in water to which garlic, onions, pepper, marjoram, salt, a bayleaf and a little wine have been added. Then leave it to soak in the liquid overnight. Next day, take out the tripe and cut it into strips and cook it together with fried onions, salt, pepper, paprika and *lecsó* (a prepared mixture of cooked green peppers and tomatoes) until done. It is at this stage that the diced pig's ears fried with onions are added, to make the dish even more tasty.

century as a description of the area inhabited by numerous outlaws, many of whom were former cattle drovers who had nowhere to turn for a living apart from soldiering as opportunity offered. They were known as "Haiduks" and their bravery in battle was a decisive factor in the victorious campaigns of István Bocskai, Prince of Transylvania, who rewarded them by settling many thousands on his estates and investing their settlements, the so-called "Haiduk towns", with the privileges of nobility.

Mária Czinege's ability to conjure up the authentic flavours of the Hajdúság stems not only from her own skills as a cook and from the recipes inherited from as far back as her great-grandmother, but also from the quality of the hams and sausages provided and prepared by the "master of the house", i.e. her husband Józsi. Until his retirement, Mr. Czinege was employed by the Post Office in Debrecen as a line-extension mechanic, but he is also an expert in the rearing of pigs and the preparation of the various delicious products obtained from them.

The first dish which Mrs. Czinege brought to the table was a soup made out of a fine tender corn-fed chicken. The recipe, she told us, came from Nagyiván, the village where she was born. (Nagyiván is one of the villages settled by István Bocskai's Haiduks after the military campaigns at the beginning of the 17th century.) In fact, it would be wrong to think of this dish merely as a soup, since, being made out of a whole chicken, it was a full meal or more in itself. Nevertheless, it turned out to be only an introduction, which was followed immediately by the chicken itself (stuffed with a mixture of egg, diced

Mária Czinege sews up the skin of the chicken (top)
A beautifully roasted stuffed chicken (right)

10

DEBRECEN STYLE DISHES

MENUS often include dishes described as "Debrecen style", meaning, for the most part, that they contain some meat product peculiar to Debrecen which gives them their special character and flavour. Take for example stuffed cabbage, which is a favourite dish throughout Hungary, but which done Debrecen style, is in my experience capable of competing with every hope of success against any other version I know.

In Debrecen, I sampled this particular dish at the Hajdúság Restaurant, next door to the theatre. The restaurant itself plays the part to a certain extent of an artists' club, since the "actors' hostel" where artists filling engagements at the theatre for shorter or longer periods are accommodated, is situated nearby. Numerous theatre people therefore spend their free time during the day at the restaurant. Before starting on the stuffed cabbage I was served a soup made out of spare-ribs (these are the long ends of the pork ribs, with their meat attached). Together with the vegetables cooked in the soup they make a substantial, appetizing dish, to which home-made

Ingredients for Debrecen stuffed cabbage (left), and the finished masterpiece (bottom)

pasta-pellets are added for cooking just before serving, and which pleasantly enhance the flavour.

The stuffed cabbage is prepared from home-made sauerkraut. The leaves for filling should be carefully chosen and of a good size, and the filling itself—apart from minced beef and pork—normally contains a certain amount of rice. Seasoning includes not only salt and black pepper, but also paprika of the "noble-sweet" variety. The particular Debrecen element of the dish is provided by the twin Debrecen sausages, which, fried nice and brown and surmounted by a jaunty "cock's comb" have pride of place on top. These twin sausages, which are made from selected meats, are a speciality of Debrecen and as may be inferred from their name, they always turn up in pairs like frankfurters, though they are much more bulky than the latter as well as being spiced and more highly flavoured generally. The cock's comb, however, belies its name: it has nothing whatever to do with the valiant fowl, being prepared from a notched rasher of bacon fried until it is well browned and curled up in the shape of a cock's comb, then it is sprinkled with paprika to make it look even more colourful.

While I was slowly making my way through the stuffed cabbage, the actors came in one after the other—not to

have dinner, but just to partake of a snack to keep hunger at bay before the performance, as I was informed by Mr. Mikáczó, the manager of the restaurant. In fact they were ordering what are known as "zone-portions"—a concept dating back to the last century and re-introduced at the restaurant by Mr. Mikáczó himself notwithstanding his youthfulness. The name came about as follows: during the expansion of the Hungarian railway network in the second half of the 19th century the then Minister of Transport, Gábor Baross, introduced the so-called "zone-tariff" which opened up the possibility of cheaper travel and was consequently extremely popular. The idea spread initially to the railway refreshment rooms, where they began to provide *zónapörkölt* (i.e. small portion of *pörkölt* for rapid consumption), and it was later adopted throughout the country in restaurants both large and small.

The Debrecen "zone-pörkölt" is generally made of mutton, a custom which no doubt originates from the fact that the mutton produced around these parts is very good indeed. When they make a *pörkölt* they first cut the meat into cubes, then they scald it, drain it, sprinkle red paprika and lightly-fried onions over the top and continue browning and braising—adding a little garlic and red wine—until the *pörkölt* is nearly done. Then they add tomatoes and peppers and continue cooking until the dish is ready. The result is an extremely tasty, unmistakably genuine Debrecen *pörkölt*.

Spare-rib soup (bottom). The fish paprika, genuine Krúdy-style (right)

IN THE STEPS OF SINDBAD

THE façade of the small, two-storey, Baroque house is decorated with a fresco faded by the passage of time. It represents a legendary figure dressed in a broad-brimmed hat, and waistcoat with metal buttons, stirring the savoury contents of a cauldron—a figure conjured here somehow from the early 20th-century world of Gyula Krúdy, who, in the person of his fictional, the Hungarian Sindbad, journeyed both in the past and in the present. The restaurant contained in this house was one of the famous author's favourite haunts during the period when he was working on a newspaper in Debrecen, and it faithfully preserves the Krúdy-tradition to this day. First and foremost in the form of the author's favourite dishes—since, as it is well known, he was a connoisseur of food and drink, and many a dish described by him is still extant in the repertoire of the restaurant's kitchen. It was here, at the Krúdy Restaurant in Debrecen, that I stumbled on a contemporary description of fish paprika, which is attributed to the author himself. It reads as follows: "Take various types of fish, cut them into pieces of the same size, leave them to stand for an hour and a half in salt, then take plenty of finely chopped onions, put them in a saucepan and sauté them lightly in butter, add a good pinch of paprika, add the fish and cook with lid on for half an hour, finally add a spoonful of water and some sour cream, bring to the boil, and serve." The fresco on the façade of the restaurant shows the preparation of a fish paprika, I am informed by the restaurateur Attila Szilágyi. He offers me some, too: it is cooked just as they used to cook it at the beginning of the century, in the genuine Krúdy-style.

There is gypsy music at the Krúdy Restaurant, faithful to the tradition of Pista Dankó, the famous gypsy band-leader and composer of songs. For more than a decade at the turn of the century Dankó played his music both here and at the Kispipa ("Little Pipe") Restaurant, making up songs which later became popular, on the spur of the moment and without recourse to written music of any kind. Of course, these made-up songs were not exactly in the same category as the pentatonic folk-songs collected by Bartók and Kodály. Nevertheless, they appealed to many people, and they continue to be sung to this day.

Let us, however, return to Krúdy's favourite food, beef, which was consumed with particular relish in Debrecen in view of the excellence of the beef cattle reared on the neighbouring Hortobágy *puszta*. So excellent were they in fact that, as Krúdy wrote in one of his sketches, during the time of the Dual Monarchy they used to be driven straight from the Hortobágy to the Hofburg in Vienna. Indeed, the Emperor Franz Josef insisted that his favourite dish—boiled beef—should be made only from Hortobágy beef.

Attila Szilágyi's method of commemorating the famous gourmet is not through a plaque or marble slab, but through the organizing of "Krúdy dinners" at the restaurant, which on these occasions becomes a place of pilgrimage for devotees not only from Debrecen itself, but also from the surrounding areas. The introductory

appetizer normally consists of marrow-bone with toasted bread, accompanied by beer fresh from the barrel. After this comes a broth made, of course, out of shin of beef, accompanied by an appropriate amount of soup bones and vegetables—the latter consisting not only of parsley root, carrots, celeriac and kohlrabi, but also of onions, tomatoes, green peppers and a segment of savoy cabbage. Add to these pepper, caraway seed, a bayleaf, and home-made pasta (made with eggs) which is a particularly palatable local speciality, and your dish is complete.

In the interests of strict historical accuracy I should mention that Krúdy's favourite dish was boiled beef, removed from the pot when tender, and served accompanied by horseradish dressed with vinegar or a tomato sauce. Attila Szilágyi needed little prodding to conjure up a sample before me, accompanied on this occasion by horseradish dressed with vinegar, the piquant flavour of which nicely complemented the taste of the beef.

Next came braised sirloin cutlet with mushrooms, forming a worthy climax to the Krúdy dinner. The well matured beef braised together with smoked bacon and mushrooms freshly gathered in the neighbouring woods, constituted an exceptionally succulent dish. Krúdy remarked in connection with it that his favourite dishes were those which achieved their effect through the natural flavours of their ingredients, and today's gourmet can only agree.

The Krúdy Restaurant (top left) and the famous author's favourite dishes: marrowbone (bottom left), steak with mushrooms (bottom right), beef broth and stewed beef (right)

"SLAMBUC" AT MRS. CSIKÓS'S

I visited Mrs. Csikós, whose cooking is spoken of with awe throughout the district, at the little farmstead near Debrecen where she lives. Nowadays she only goes into town on special occasions to cook, mostly when old acquaintances turn up and insist on her preparing the meal. Otherwise she tends to remain at home, cooking for the family, or for friends who pay her a visit especially to sample her bean goulash and the famous dish of the herdsmen—"slambuc". There are a number of closely guarded secrets when it comes to the preparation of a bean goulash—as Mrs. Csikós confided to me—and the main one is that you must use a special type of mottled bean known as "Jewish beans". These may have got their name from their use in the preparation of *sólet* (a dish of barley and beans) which is traditionally associated with the Jews. The meat ingredient is topside of beef, but, again, not just any will do: it must be the very best, boneless, meat. As for the onions, vegetables and parsley which go to make the goulash, these she grows in her own garden. However, the most important thing is that the goulash must, under all circumstances, be cooked over an open fire in a cauldron well seasoned by use and age.

Fortunately there was still a little bean goulash left over from the midday meal as a taster. As it is well known, bean goulash and stuffed cabbage are the two exceptions to the rule, both taste better warmed up than when first served; so I gladly sampled a few spoonfuls before asking

Mrs. Csikós to cook me a dish of *slambuc*, the famous dish of the herdsmen. I wanted to see how it was done, from beginning to end.

Slambuc is a dish of great antiquity, and it exists in various forms in other parts of the Alföld, where it remains popular.

Mrs. Csikós gladly set to work preparing the dish, partly because she already had some of her own home-made flat noodles to hand and these are the main prerequisite. Also, the weather was suitable for the cooking to be done in a cauldron over an open fire, which is just as important in the case of a *slambuc* as it is for a goulash. She set to therefore without hesitation: first she diced some smoked bacon, tossed it into the cauldron, and when the fat began to melt in the heat from the flames, she added some finely chopped onions to brown in it. Next she added the flat noodles and browned them too, stirring continuously. After sprinkling some red paprika and salt over the top, she added the diced potatoes, which had to be cooked in with the noodles, and finally she added a little water. Now and again she gave the cauldron a good shake to prevent the contents catching on the bottom and to ensure that they cooked evenly. "You must never stir at this point," she remarked emphatically. "The secret of a good *slambuc* is the way you shake it."

I resolved there and then that I would never, never stir a *slambuc* while it was cooking—should I ever, by any chance, wish to prepare this famous dish. How it would turn out if I did, I have no means of telling, but one thing

Ingredients for "slambuc", the famous dish of the herdsmen (top) and Mrs. Csikós's cheese-curd turnover (left)

at least is certain: done "Mrs. Csikós-style" it is indeed delicious. True, however, it is not exactly the dish if you are trying to lose weight.

In this connection I was, moreover, exposed to further temptation. After all that had gone before, I was now confronted with some superb curd cheese pastries which I really should have declined, but it would not have been easy to put up a successful resistance.

They consisted of a sort of curd cheese turnover, which is a very excellent, and fairly well known, pastry. You make a leavened dough in the usual way, then you make a filling out of a mixture of curd cheese, lemon flavoured egg-yolk, raisins, and vanilla flavoured sugar, and use it to fill the rolled out dough cut into squares and folded over the top. The pastry is really excellent, flaky and feather-light the way Mrs. Csikós makes it, and the filling is delicious too. But this was not the last of the surprises that my hostess had in store for me. When making the turnovers, after folding the corners of the squares of dough over the filling, she put some of them to one side, instead of placing them in the oven with the remainder to bake. Then she heated some oil in a frying pan and fried the turnovers which she had put aside in boiling oil, like doughnuts. It was a pleasant surprise: no sooner had I disposed of the first "turnover-doughnut" than the second followed, and then the third, before (calories or not!) I was able to bring myself to a halt.

OX-ROASTS

JÓZSEF Kölbl belongs to the older generation of Debrecen chefs. There was a time when he used to be employed by the best restaurants in town, but now he teaches future chefs at the college of the catering trade.
The old chef has a hobby which has made his name famous well beyond the bounds of Debrecen. József Kölbl's favourite occupation is roasting oxen on the spit, a task which he not only undertakes with pleasure, but, being possessed of certain secrets known only to himself, does it with such artistry, that the flesh of the huge animal revolving on the spit becomes marvellously tender and delicious under the master's hand.

Spit-roasted ox, since ancient times, has been a favoured accompaniment to popular festivities in Hungary, and there still exists a recipe compiled by a chef in times long past, according to which the flesh of an ox roasted on the spit will be truly succulent only if the ox has first been stuffed with a deer, the deer with a sucking-pig, and the sucking-pig with a chicken. Then the whole lot has to be roasted over a slow fire, turning the spit carefully so that the meat cooks evenly on every side.

A roasted ox is traditionally the favourite accompaniment to folk festivals in Hungary (top). Antal Láng, master cooper, at the Hortobágy-bridge market (left)

According to József Kölbl, while the mediaeval chef in question no doubt obtained excellent results by this method, it seems likely that those with access to the well-cooked, tender, "inside meat" would have fared better than those obliged to whittle away layer upon layer of the outside—which probably roasted for longer (and turned out tougher) than it should have done.

József Kölbl has brought the old method of roasting an ox on a spit up to date, in accordance with his own ideas. Whenever he is invited anywhere to perform this function—and that happens very often—he first of all selects a prime beef animal, which is duly slaughtered two or three days before the roasting is scheduled to take place, in order to give time for the flesh to mature in cold storage. No large fire is required for the roasting—just live coals. First of all the ox is larded with bacon, then it is drawn on to the spit, and given a quarter turn every half an hour as the roasting continues. Naturally, this is easier to describe than to accomplish, since it takes four men to turn the huge animal on the spit, and they also have to watch very carefully, to make sure that it turns evenly and browns uniformly over the coals. Nowadays no one stuffs the ox with a deer, sucking-pig, or any other animal, and Mr. Kölbl's method of producing superbly tender, succulent roast beef, is to carve it off in layers as it cooks, place the slices on onion rings browned in fat, season with garlic and marjoram, pour on a little red wine, and then braise thoroughly. In this way the meat

not only turns out tender, but it also acquires an excellent aroma and flavour.

The only thing that remains to be clarified is where and when one can take part in an ox-roast, since not only is it of interest from a gourmet's point of view, but it is also a spectacle well out of the ordinary, accompanied, as it invariably is, by different forms of merry-making and entertainment, for example gypsy music and dancing. As I have already mentioned, József Kölbl undertakes several ox-roasts annually. For example, he receives invitations to vintage celebrations, or to the Normafa Restaurant in Budapest to roast an ox for the benefit of the hordes of tourists which throng the capital. So there is only one reliable tip which I can give: on the Hortobágy *puszta,* on the occasion of the "bridge fair", which takes place on 19th and 20th August, it is unlikely that an ox-roast will fail to form part of the proceedings. Over many hundreds of years it has been the tradition for thousands of people to converge on the bridge from all corners of the Alföld, near and far, at the time of the fair—whether for buying and selling, or just to watch and enjoy themselves. Originally it was a market for cattle and other livestock, but later the various craftsmen began to put in an appearance with their wares, followed by the people who sold grilled sausages, and others who erected stalls and cooked hot meals. Then there were the showmen of various kinds, and the musicians. To this day the "bridge fair" remains a colourful, animated scene, and anyone who decides to visit the Hortobágy over the period may be sure of sampling a portion of roast ox!

Farmstead on the Hortobágy (bottom). The market at the bridge still presents a colourful animated scene: here you may find vendors of honey cakes and törökméz *(a favourite sweet-*

meat), gypsies with their home-made wooden tubs, expert sieve-makers, herdsmen taking the opportunity of a snack—or just watching; bird-fanciers, and even a merry-go-round (right)

INNS ON THE HORTOBÁGY

THOUGH it lies in the immediate vicinity of Debrecen, the Hortobágy is nevertheless a different world. If you stand for the first time on the "nine-span bridge", and look around you at the endless plain, all you will see is a single mighty expanse of open land, the monotony of which is broken only by the occasional herd of cattle, flock of sheep, or distant clump of trees. Later, however, it emerges that the *puszta* is full of life. When one gets to know it better, it is apparent that each part of it has a different aspect. The Hortobágy shows one of its moods, for example, over there, where the glossy-coated chestnut horses of the stud are galloping to and fro; and another, over there, where the grey, long-horned "Hungarian breed" cattle are making their way to the drinking trough beside the draw-well. Again, a further mood is shown by a distant white patch on the plain, denoting the presence of thousands—perhaps tens of thousands—of geese, and yet another by a flash of blue from the surface of the fish ponds. The greater part of the *puszta* has been preserved in its original form as a nature reserve: the Hortobágy National Park extends over an area of fifty-two thousand hectares, and represents a haven for rare plants and wild-life threatened with extinction. Here lie undisturbed the

Cattle grazing on the Hortobágy (page before)
The inn at Kadarcs (top and left)

24

swamps and marshy tracts which serve as resting-places for mallard and wild geese during the spring and autumn migrations; and there are stretches of woodland in which red-footed falcons, eagle-owls, and grey shrikes have their nests. There are soda lakes, too, with their characteristic plant and wild-life.

The Hortobágy, as may be inferred from the above, was not always a wilderness. At the beginning of the 13th century it supported more than fifty settlements according to contemporary records, out of which twelve are described as having their own churches. The depopulation of the area began with the Mongol invasion in 1241, and later the increasing alkalinity resulting from deforestation, together with unfavourable changes in the climate and soil conditions led to gradual abandonment by the remaining population. Two hundred years after the Mongol invasion, at the end of the 15th century, the documents already refer to the Hortobágy as *puszta* (wasteland), and the town of Debrecen temporary expropriation of depopulated areas, then through absorption into permanent ownership.

One should perhaps point out that Debrecen and the surrounding district survived the century and a half of Turkish occupation relatively unscathed. Even in hard times the citizens were able to continue the pursuit of their peaceful occupations—handicrafts, commerce, and the breeding of livestock, this last being one of the prin-

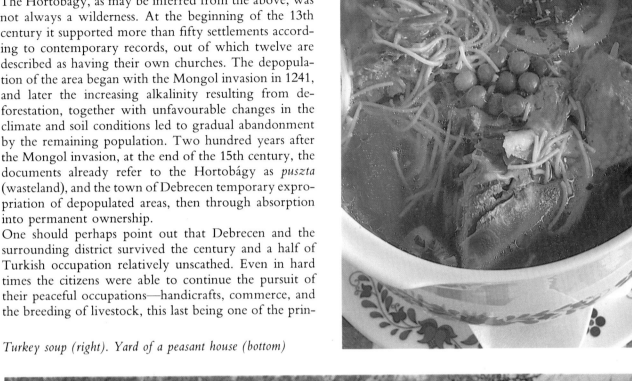

Turkey soup (right). Yard of a peasant house (bottom)

25

One of the Hortobágy Inn's famous dishes; the Hortobágy pancake (top). Baked rice, garnished with roast goose-legs (left). Goose farm on the puszta *(right)*

cipal sources of income of the town. Initially animals were reared on free range ("in the wild", as the expression went) both summer and winter. In later centuries, however, with the introduction of winter stabling, this practice only prevailed in part. In the course of time, part of the Hortobágy came to be used not only for pasture, but also in the form of allotments, which the town of Debrecen leased for agricultural purposes to the inhabitants of the neighbouring villages. Unfortunately these arrangements came to an end during the 19th century. As a result of the regulation of the waters of the Tisza the water-table was gradually lowered, the fertile silt was no longer deposited, and the soil became progressively more alkaline and unsuitable for cultivation. Since then there have been various attempts to put the Hortobágy to productive use. Fish ponds were excavated, experiments were undertaken with the cultivation of rice, grazing land was put under the plough, and irrigation was introduced with the construction of the Eastern and Western canals. Results were mixed. The fish farms continue to breed fish successfully, but the production of rice and other crops needing irrigation has not proved economical. As the locals say "the *puszta* wants to remain a *puszta*", and perhaps it is better so, since, apart from the

Bugac *puszta* near Kecskemét, only the Hortobágy is left of the legendary *puszta*s of olden times. It has been designated as a National Park, where both the natural environment and the intimate connection between stock-rearing by traditional methods and the ancient rural occupations and way of life in general, have been preserved for present and future generations.

Proceeding from Debrecen in the direction of the Hortobágy, we arrived at the Kadarcs *Csárda* (inn) on the eastern edge of the *puszta*. The old "smoky kitchen" has been done up to look like the original, though it is not in use, since cooking now takes place in a modern kitchen. The premises have been fitted out with hand-carved furnishings, made by a rural craftsman, and the food served in the inn is in keeping with the atmosphere too, particularly the dishes prepared from poultry bred on the Hortobágy farms. The turkey soup served as first course clearly owed much of its excellence to the fact that it was made from a corn-fed bird reared locally; though doubtless the delicious vegetables in it, grown in the kitchen garden of the inn, contributed their share also. The roast lamb which followed proved to be a worthy successor!

An important commercial route crossed the Hortobágy in olden times. Though never as famous as the Amber Route of the Romans, which cut across present-day western Hungary, it was nevertheless of considerable importance in its own way, since it was the route followed by valuable livestock on their way to the markets of the west. The inns built along the road were spaced at distances which could be covered comfortably during the course of one day by a herd on the move. Every inn had its draw-well and watering trough for the animals—as well as pasture, of course, since the entire Hortobágy consisted of one vast stretch of grazing land—while the drovers could expect a hot meal, and something to drink with it.

The former day's journey has now been reduced to a short trip in a motor car. Less than half-an-hour's run brought us to the end of the next stage, and it only took that long because we drove slowly, stopping every now and then to have a closer look for example at a barking, black *puli* dog rounding up a flock of sheep, while the shepherd stood by quietly watching the intelligent animal doing his work for him. Or, later, at a thatched lean-to, surrounded by an ocean of white geese, stretching as far as the eye could see. This particular stage is marked by the inn next to the nine-span bridge, which has been mentioned previously. A porticoed, old-fashioned house, stork's nest on the roof, tables with brightly-coloured tablecloths in front—this is the famous Hortobágy Inn, right in the middle of the *puszta*.

The Hortobágy Inn is an ancient traditional place for travellers to rest and refresh themselves with food and drink. The earliest written mention of it dates back to 1699, when the town of Debrecen established an inn in the heart of the *puszta*. The 17th-century folk-Baroque style, colonnaded building was enlarged in the 19th century by the addition of a wing in the Neo-Classic style, and it has remained the same to this day—preserving memories of the writers, poets and painters, who tarried for shorter or longer periods within its walls, seeking their inspiration from the *puszta*.

The inn and its surroundings have nowadays become a tourist centre, with exhibitions, picture and sculpture-galleries, and souvenir vendors. Fortunately, the inn itself has preserved something of the old traditions: there are superb "Hortobágy dishes" to be found on the menu.

For first course Géza Nagy, the innkeeper, provided "herdsmen's soup", containing diced beef, smoked bacon, onions, mixed vegetables, *lecsó* (mixed tomatoes and peppers), and *tarhonya* (dried pasta pellets). It was

delicious. Then the conversation turned to the question of the famous Hortobágy pancake, which, we were told, exists in two versions. Both call for the pancake to be filled with either veal *pörkölt* or paprika chicken, and flavoured with pepper, sour cream, caraway seeds and paprika, but at this point the two versions part company. One is served as it is, with a *pörkölt* and sour cream sauce poured over it, but the other is dipped in flour, beaten egg and breadcrumbs, fried, and served accompanied by tartar sauce. Thanks to the kindness of our host, both versions appeared on the table, but I was unable to make up my mind which I liked better, however much I sampled them. The version with the sour cream sauce goes further and is more filling, while the other one— fried and served with tartar sauce—is lighter and more highly flavoured. Later it emerged that this dish, which is known throughout Hungary as a "Hortobágy pancake", originated, after all, not out on the Hortobágy, but back in Debrecen. It was invented by a former chef at the Golden Bull, Béla Henrik, around the turn of the century.

I would never have thought that lambs' brains done in egg and breadcrumbs and served with fried potatoes and tartar sauce could be so delicious. When I go on to mention that, after this, I also sampled a small portion of deliciously crisp roast goose, it will scarcely be necessary to explain what an effort it was to turn my attention to the speciality of the house, the "Hortobágy platter"

The Hortobágy horse herd and the csikós *(herdsman) in charge of them*

29

which was served immediately afterwards. When I tasted it, it became apparent that the secret of the "Hortobágy platter" lies in the combination of flavours represented by the pork cutlets, Debrecen sausage, onions and smoked bacon. Between each pair of well-beaten, peppered, boned pork cutlets is inserted the filling made of smoked bacon cut into strips, onions, and chopped Debrecen sausage. Then the cutlets are pinned together, dipped in flour mixed with paprika, and fried in oil, so that all the various flavours blend most appetizingly during the cooking. It is perhaps scarcely necessary to mention that the dish emphatically calls for a good wine to be served with it. As far as I was concerned, I followed my usual practice and ordered a local wine. The wines grown on the sandy soils of the Alföld are somewhat lighter and less full-bodied than the hill-slope wines of the traditional wine-producing areas, but their freshness and pleasant bouquet make up for this in ample measure.

Subsequently our route led across the bridge, which rests on nine vaulted arches (hence the popular name for it "the bridge with nine holes"). It was constructed at the beginning of the last century. A few kilometres on the other side of the bridge lies Máta, the home of the Hortobágy stud farm. From time to time riding-displays and carriage-driving competitions are held there, including the traditional Debrecen five-in-hand, and herdsmen wearing their broad-brimmed *hajdú* hats performing feats of daring on horseback.

Beyond the fish ponds I came across another inn on the edge of the *puszta*. It is named after one of the outlaws of days gone by, Bandi Patkó, whose favourite inn this was, at least that is how the legend runs, which also has it that he levied his contributions only on the rich, while he gave to the poor. As a result he had many followers and helpers, who hid him and kept him informed of the whereabouts of the pursuing gendarmes.

At the Bandi Patkó Inn I was served with traditional Hortobágy dishes. First, mutton goulash, cooked in a cauldron outside in the yard and containing *galuska* noodles (gnocchi) cooked in the goulash itself, as is customary around these parts. Next, "Hajdúság pork slices", consisting of slices of pork well beaten, rolled up, filled with some kind of home-made sausage, fried until nice and brown, and served garnished with braised cabbage. Since the Tisza is quite near here, the inn usually has fish on the menu, and on this particular day the main attraction was a *harcsa* (sheat-fish) *pörkölt*. The local fishermen had brought in a good-sized *harcsa*, which had been used in the preparation of this appetizing dish, the aroma and flavour of which are enhanced by the sour cream sauce in which the portions of fish are served. The gentle, clear waters of the Tisza, the many subtleties of the sunny Alföld—all these are to be experienced in this simple, yet ingenious dish, which is so typical of the best of Hungarian cuisine.

The Patkó Inn where the old-style peasant oven is still to be seen (top left). Some good-sized sheat-fish caught by Tisza fishermen (bottom left). Mutton pörkölt only tastes right, they say, when it is cooked in a cauldron over an open fire (right)

Nightfall on the puszta *(following page)*

30

THE RECIPES OF THE HORTOBÁGY REGION

by Mari Lajos

HORTOBÁGY PANCAKES (HORTOBÁGYI HÚSOS PALACSINTA)

For the filling:
400 g (14 oz) veal or lean pork
1 large onion
1 green pepper
1 tomato
50 g (2 oz) smoked bacon
1 tsp paprika (not too hot)
300 ml (½ pt) sour cream (or fresh cream)
10 g (½ oz) flour
parsley
salt
For the pancakes:
200 g (7 oz) flour
2 eggs
200 ml (⅓ pt) milk
200 ml (⅓ pt) approx. of soda water or similar
2 tbsp oil
salt

Mix together the ingredients to obtain a salty pancake batter. Leave it to stand for 1 hour, then use it to make thin pancakes (2 per person). Meanwhile prepare the filling, that is the *pörkölt,* as follows: dice the smoked bacon and fry it until the fat becomes transparent. Now add the finely chopped onions and braise under a lid until tender. Remove from the stove, sprinkle with the paprika powder, and add the meat cut into medium-sized cubes. Fry for a few minutes over high heat, stirring continuously, then reduce the heat. Add the green pepper, the tomato, and salt to taste, and continue cooking with the lid on until tender. Remove the meat from the gravy, cut it up very small; meanwhile add the sour cream and flour smoothly mixed together to the gravy in the pan and bring to the boil. Add enough of the mixture to the meat to obtain a filling which spreads easily, and use this to fill the pancakes. Fold them over, tucking in the ends, and then place them side by side in a fireproof dish. Pour the remainder of the gravy and sour cream mixture over the top, and place in a pre-heated, medium oven. Remove when piping hot, decorate with parsley, and serve immediately, accompanied by additional sour cream in a separate bowl, if you wish.

SPARE-RIB SOUP (ORJALEVES)

800 g (1¾ lb) pork spare-ribs
500 g (1 lb 2 oz) mixed soup vegetables
    (carrots, turnip, celery, kohlrabi)
1 medium onion
2 cloves garlic
10–15 peppercorns
a tiny bit of cherry-pepper
1 level tsp of saffron
1 bunch parsley
150 g (5 oz) savoy cabbage
1 green pepper
1 tomato
100–150 g (4–5 oz) small pasta shells

Put the chopped up spare-ribs into cold water to cover and bring to the boil. Add the pepper-corns, garlic, piece of cherry-pepper and the saffron all enclosed in a tea-infuser (tea-egg), then the whole onion also and a little salt. Simmer gently for half an hour without a lid, then add the mixed vegetables cut into half-inch pieces, together with the kohlrabi, green pepper and tomato whole. Continue cooking until both meat and vegetables are tender. Now remove the onion, kohlrabi, green pepper, tomato and the infuser from the soup, and skim any surplus fat off the surface. Cook the pasta in slightly salted water in a separate pan, drain it, and add to soup. Add more salt if necessary and sprinkle chopped parsley over the top on serving.

COUNTRY SOUP (FALUSI LEVES)

750 g (1 lb 10 oz) mixed meats (leg of pork, shin of beef, boned chicken-breast)
300 g (10 oz) mixed vegetables (carrots, turnip, celery, kohlrabi)
100 g (4 oz) green beans
100 g (4 oz) pickled gherkins
100 g (4 oz) champignons
100 g (4 oz) potatoes
1 medium onion
1 clove of garlic
1 tbsp oil or fat
1 tsp paprika
1 small bunch of parsley
salt
pepper
For the pastry:
300 g (10 oz) flour
15 g (½ oz) yeast
150 ml (¼ pt) milk
1 small cube of sugar
1 egg
2 tbsp oil
salt
1 egg yolk for glazing

33

Fry the finely chopped onion in the oil until crisp and sprinkle with paprika. Turn the mixed meats cut into strips in it, pour in 1½ l (2½ pts) of cold water and season with a little salt. Simmer slowly with a lid on for 30 minutes. Now add the thinly sliced mixed vegetables, the chopped green beans, pickled gherkins, mushrooms and potatoes, the garlic, and ground pepper to taste. Simmer slowly, covered, until all the ingredients are tender. Add further salt if necessary.

While the soup is cooking, prepare the pastry as follows: liquefy the yeast in the lukewarm milk sweetened with the small cube of sugar. Add this to the flour, oil, egg, with salt to taste, and knead thoroughly. Form the dough into a loaf, sprinkle flour over the top, cover it over with a kitchen cloth and leave it in a warmish place to double its bulk. When risen, knead again gently, cutting the dough into four pieces, and stretch them out into circular shapes.

When the soup is done, remove the garlic and pour the soup evenly into 4 fairly deep small fire-proof dishes or casseroles. Sprinkle parsley over the top and stand them in a baking tray. Seal with the circular sheets of dough, brush over with the egg to glaze the pastry, and bake in a hot (200°C) preheated oven for 20–25 minutes until nice and brown on top. Remove the casseroles from the oven, place them on saucers, and serve immediately.

This is a very substantial soup, so you will only need a very light main course to follow.

TURKEY SOUP
(PULYKALEVES)
(serves 6, 8 or 10 people, depending on the size of the bird)

1 young turkey
1 kg (2 lb 3 oz) mixed vegetables (carrots, turnip, kohlrabi, celery)
1 large onion
4-5 cloves of garlic
200 g (7 oz) of savoy cabbage
1 green pepper
1 tomato
50 g (2 oz) champignons
200 g (7 oz) cooked green peas
parsley
100 g (3 ½ oz) vermicelli
salt
peppercorns

Clean and wash the turkey. Cut it into pieces of the size you need for your guests. Put the pieces into a large saucepan and pour on sufficient water to cover well. Bring to the boil, then turn down the heat and simmer slowly without a lid, adding a little salt, peppercorns to taste, the garlic and the whole onion. When the meat begins to be tender, add the vegetables cleaned and cut into fairly large pieces. Add also the tomato, the green pepper, and the whole mushrooms, and continue cooking until all the ingredients are tender. (Meanwhile, cook the peas in a small amount of salty water in a separate saucepan). Remove the pieces of turkey from the soup

and skin them and get rid of the tendons and larger bones. Cut them into fairly small pieces, and place them in a soup-tureen. Add the soup vegetables, the peas, the vermicelli cooked in a small quantity of the soup in a separate saucepan, and the mushrooms, sliced. Strain the soup over the top. Serve piping hot, sprinkled with chopped parsley if you wish.

Note: Instead of the vermicelli you may use semolina *galuskas* (similar to gnocchi) or dumplings made out of the turkey liver.

SEMOLINA GALUSKAS
(for adding to soups)
(DARAGALUSKA)
100 g (4 oz) semolina
50 g (2 oz) butter
1 egg
salt

Whisk together the egg and the butter. Season with salt, then add the semolina and mix well together. Cover over, and leave to stand for at least an hour.

Dip a tablespoon in slightly salty boiling water or stock and use it to scoop out oblong pieces of semolina dough and to drop them into the boiling liquid. Simmer under a lid for about 15 minutes until they are done.

If you are cooking them in salty water, drain them before adding them to your previously prepared soup.

Note: You may also mix a little ground pepper and chopped parsley in with the dough, if you wish.

SLAMBUC

50 g (2 oz) smoked bacon
1 medium onion
1 tsp slightly hot paprika
200 g (7 oz) **lebbencs** (thin pasta cut into irregular squares) or **csusza** (flat noodles)
500 g (1 lb) potatoes
100 g (4 oz) paprika sausage
1 green pepper
1 tomato
salt

Dice the bacon and fry it in its own fat. Add the pasta after crumbling it a little and brown it gently. Stir in the finely chopped onion and fry it a little, then sprinkle with paprika and sufficient cold water to cover the pasta. When the pasta is partly done, add the peeled, diced potatoes, the green pepper and tomato (whole). Season with salt to taste, and when the potatoes are partly done, add the sausage cut into thin rings. Continue cooking over medium heat until all the ingredients are tender. Theoretically, you should only shake—but never stir— the pan (or cauldron if cooking over an open fire).

Note: When the dish is ready it should be "thick enough to stand a wooden spoon in", as the locals say.

ROAST STUFFED CHICKEN AND CHICKEN SOUP
(LEVESBEN FŐTT, TÖLTÖTT SÜLT TYÚK)
(serves 4-6 people)

For the soup:
1 young chicken weighing about 1½ kg (3 ½ lb)
300 g (10 oz) mixed soup vegetables
1 medium onion
2 cloves garlic
1 green pepper
1 tomato
200 g (7 oz) savoy cabbage
salt
peppercorns
1 pinch of saffron
For the stuffing:
4 hard-boiled eggs
150 g (95 oz) champignon
60 g (2 oz) semolina
1 raw egg
1 small onion
knob of butter the size of a walnut
the liver of the chicken
a pinch of marjoram
salt, pepper
1 bunch parsley
Further ingredients:
50 g (2 oz) smoked bacon
1 kg (2 lb 3 oz) peeled potatoes
2-3 tbsp oil or fat
50 ml (2 fl oz) light ale
1 tsp honey
barbecue spices

Clean the chicken, salt the stomach cavity, and leave it to stand for half an hour.
Prepare the stuffing as follows: finely chop the onion and fry it in the butter. Add the finely chopped mushrooms and season with salt and pepper.
Braise until tender, then leave to cool. Now mix in the mashed chicken-liver, the diced hard-boiled eggs, the semolina, the raw egg, the chopped parsley, and more salt and pepper as necessary.
Work all the ingredients well together, then stuff the stomach cavity with the mixture (not too firmly), also stuffing under the loosened skin of the breast. Carefully stitch up the neck and stomach cavities, place the chicken in a fair-sized cooking-pot, and pour in sufficient water to cover it. Bring to the boil, add a little salt, the soup vegetables cut into pieces, together with the onion, paprika, tomato and savoy cabbage. Add also the garlic, peppercorns and saffron—in fact everything neccessary for a good soup, and simmer without a lid over low heat. When the chicken is about half done, remove from the soup, taking care not to damage the skin. Continue cooking until the soup is done and ready to serve as your frist course. Meanwhile, cut the smoked bacon into thin slices, lay them in the bottom of a fairly deep baking pan, place the chicken on top, sprinkle with a little salt, and barbecue spices to taste (e.g. thyme, rosemary, ground aniseed, pepper etc.). Baste with the oil or melted fat and place the diced potatoes around it. Salt again, and brush over the chicken with the beer and honey mixture. Place in a preheated oven and roast at medium heat (200° C) until the chicken is nice and brown, and the potatoes are cooked through and golden yellow in colour. Serve in the pan in which it was baked, accompanied by pickles, apple-sauce, and prunes stewed in wine.

HARCSA (SHEAT-FISH) PÖRKÖLT WITH SOUR CREAM
(TEJFÖLÖS HARCSAPAPRIKÁS)

800 g (1¾ lb) boned sheat-fish
50 g (2 oz) smoked bacon
30 g (1 oz) oil or fat
1 large onion
1 tsp slightly hot paprika
2 fleshy green peppers
1 fairly large tomato
200-300 ml (¼-½ pt) sour cream
10 g (½ oz) flour
salt

Clean the fish as necessary, cut it into cubes and sprinkle lightly with salt.
Dice the smoked bacon and fry it in its own fat. Remove the cracklings from the pan, add the oil or fat to the bacon fat in the pan and fry the finely chopped onion until transparent. Remove the pan from the stove, mix in the paprika, and thin with a little water. Boil the mixture until the onion is completely reduced to a pulp. Now add the fish, the peeled tomato cut into segments, one of the finely chopped, cored green peppers, and cook, covered, for 15-20 minutes over low heat until the contents are tender (do not on any account stir them!). Finally add the sour cream mixed with the flour, bring to the boil again, and season with salt if necessary. Serve piping hot, decorated with slices of green pepper and garnished with buttered *galuska*s (gnocchi) or potatoes sprinkled with parsley.

GOOSE WITH BAKED RICE
(LUDASKÁSA)

4 medium sized goose-legs (or 2 breasts,
    or 1 kg (2 lb 3 oz) giblets
400 g (14 oz) mixed soup vegetables
1 medium sized onion
2 cloves of garlic
150 g (5 oz) polished rice
peppercorns
salt

Carefully clean the meat and place it in water to cover. Bring to the boil, add the whole onion, peppercorns as desired, enclosed together with the garlic in an infuser (tea-ball). Season lightly with salt, and continue cooking over low heat. After half an hour add the cleaned, finely chopped vegetables, and continue cooking until the meat is almost tender, but is still not coming away from the bone. Carefully remove the meat from the liquid, and while it is still hot, score the skin in a pattern of squares. Place the meat in the oven and roast it in its own dripping (brush the meat over with a mixture of honey and beer if you like) until the skin is crisp and brown.
Get rid of the contents of the tea-ball and the onion and skim any surplus fat from the surface of the stock. Place a layer of rice in a fire-proof dish and pour the stock over it. Cover the dish, and place in a preheated oven to bake until the rice is cooked (do not stir more than once, at half-time, otherwise the rice will become sticky). Serve immediately in the same fireproof dish or in another, heated dish, with the goose-legs on top. Accompany with braised red cabbage, pickles, or mixed salad.
Note: You can make the dish richer by adding 100 g (4 oz) of peas and 100 g (4 oz) of mushrooms, in which case add them when cooking the rice as they do not need to be boiled beforehand.

SMOKED PORK, SAUERKRAUT, AND BEANS
(BABOS KÁPOSZTA)

600 g (1 lb 6 oz) smoked pork, on the bone,
    (knuckle or thin flank)
500 g (1 lb 2 oz) sauerkraut
250 g (9 oz) mottled beans
1 large onion
1 bayleaf
300 g (1 oz) fat
50 g (2 oz) flour
1 tsp paprika
salt
pepper

Soak the beans and meat separately in lukewarm water overnight. Next day put the pork knuckle in cold water to cover and bring it to the boil. When it is partially tender, add the beans (after rinsing them) and the bayleaf. Continue cooking until all the ingredients are tender. Remove the meat from the pan, bone it while it is still hot, and cut it into little pieces.

Meanwhile, lightly rinse the sauerkraut and cook it in a small amount of water together with the onion cut into rings. When tender mix together the beans, sauerkraut and meat in a good-sized cooking-pot. Brown the flour in the fat and remove from the stove. Sprinkle with the paprika, add 100 ml (4 fl oz) of cold water and mix until smooth. Then add the mixture to the beans and sauerkraut in the cooking-pot and cook together until done. Season with salt and freshly ground pepper, remove the bayleaf, and the dish is ready to serve.

MUTTON PÖRKÖLT
(BIRKAPÖRKÖLT)

1 kg (2 lb 3 oz) leg or shoulder of mutton (boned)
100 g (4 oz) lard (or oil)
150 g (5 oz) onions
2 tsp paprika
1 green pepper
1 tomato
salt
1 clove of garlic

Remove the fat carefully from the meat, and wash the meat itself several times in water (changing the water each time). Then cut it into 2 cm (¾ in) cubes. Finely chop the onions and fry them in the lard (or oil). Remove the pan from the stove, sprinkle with the paprika and add the meat. Brown over high heat, stirring continuously until most of the liquid has evaporated. Now add the finely chopped green pepper and tomato, the crushed clove of garlic, and season lightly with salt. Cook, under cover over medium heat until the meat is tender.
Serve garnished with galuska (gnocchi), and accompanied by pickles if you wish.

BEAN GOULASH
(BABGULYÁS)

For the pörkölt:
400 g (14 oz) shin of beef (rump or chuck)
1 large onion
2 tbsp oil or fat
1 tsp paprika
1 green pepper
1 tomato
salt
Further ingredients:
250 g (9 oz) mottled beans
200 g (8 oz) smoked pork (e.g. knuckle, spare flank, etc.)
1 clove garlic
1 bayleaf
salt
parsley
200 ml (8 fl oz) sour cream
bunch of dill

Use the ingredients given to make a beef *pörkölt* in the same way as described in the recipe for mutton *pörkölt*. On the previous evening wash the smoked pork, check over your beans, and put them in to soak separately overnight. Next day rinse the smoked pork, place it in cold water together with the bayleaf and the garlic, and put it on to cook. About half way through the cooking add the beans, after rinsing and draining them, and continue cooking until all the ingredients are tender.

Remove the meat from the pan, bone it if necessary, then dice it. Get rid of the bayleaf and the garlic and drain the beans. Add them, together with the diced smoked meat, to the *pörkölt*. Salt according to taste and boil together until well blended.

Serve sprinkled with parsley, and accompany with sour cream mixed with chopped dill, in a separate bowl.

DEBRECEN STUFFED CABBAGE (DEBRECENI TÖLTÖTT KÁPOSZTA)

1 kg (2 lb 3 oz) sauerkraut
8 whole sauerkraut leaves
400 g (14 oz) minced pork
100 g (4 oz) parboiled rice
2 medium onions
1 clove garlic
2 tsp noble-sweet paprika
1 egg
ground caraway seeds
marjoram
50 g (2 oz) smoked bacon
2 pairs of Debrecen sausages
2 tbsp oil or fat
200–300 ml (¼–½ pt) sour cream
salt
pepper

Dice the smoked bacon, fry it and add to the minced meat. Fry the finely chopped onions in the bacon fat until crisp. Add half of them to the minced meat, take the pan off the heat and sprinkle the remaining onions with 1 teaspoon of paprika and a little water. Rinse the shredded sauerkraut a little, set half of it aside, and mix the onion and paprika mixture into the remainder.

Prepare the filling as follows: Cut the thick ribs out of the sauerkraut leaves. Mix together the minced meat, rice, crushed clove of garlic, egg, 1 teaspoon paprika, salt, pepper, ground caraway seeds and dried marjoram, and work well together. Spread the filling evenly but not too firmly over the sauerkraut leaves. Fold the edges of the leaves over the filling, roll them into a cylindrical shape, and lay them on the bed of sauerkraut which you have already prepared, together with the sausages. Cover with the remainder of the sauerkraut. Cook, covered, over low heat, shaking the pan occasionally until done.

Now remove the stuffed sauerkraut leaves from the pan (carefully, so that they don't fall to pieces), and the sausages also. Brown the flour in the oil or fat and mix it together with 100 ml (4 fl oz) of cold water (do not let it form any lumps). Add it to the sauerkraut and boil thoroughly. Notch the Debrecen sausages. Put the stuffed leaves back into the shredded sauerkraut, add the Debrecen sausages and pour a little sour cream over the top. Serve piping hot. You can mix a little chopped dill in with the sour cream if you wish.

DEBRECEN TOKÁNY (STEW) (DEBRECENI TOKÁNY)

600 g (1 lb 6 oz) beef chuck
100 g (4 oz) smoked bacon
1 large onion
200 g (8 oz) Debrecen sausage
150 g (5 oz) **lecsó** (a prepared mixture of cooked green peppers and tomatoes)
    or 2 green peppers and 2 tomatoes
1 clove garlic
1 tsp paprika
salt
pepper

Dice the smoked bacon and fry it. Fry the finely chopped onion in the bacon fat until crisp, add the meat after cutting it into finger-thick strips 4-5 cm (1½–2 in) long. Continue frying for a few minutes, then remove the pan from the stove. Sprinkle with the paprika and season with salt and pepper to taste. Stew, covered, in its own gravy over low heat. When it is nearly done, add the crushed garlic, the *lecsó* (or the finely chopped green peppers and tomatoes), and the sliced Debrecen sausage. Continue stewing with the lid on until all the ingredients are done. Serve accompanied by boiled rice and *tarhonya* (dried pellets of dough).

Note: Another version of this dish is made with lean leg of pork, in which case it should be served with fried potatoes tossed in the gravy in the pan.

BRAISED SIRLOIN STEAKS (SERPENYŐS ROSTÉLYOS)

4 sirloin steaks (each 200 g—½ lb)
100 g (4 oz) oil or fat
200 g (8 oz) onions
20 g (1½ oz) paprika
200 g (8 oz) green peppers
100 g (4 oz) tomatoes
1 kg (2 lb 3 oz) potatoes
1 clove garlic
salt
caraway seeds
a little flour
parsley

Beat the steaks out a little and notch their edges. Season with salt, dip in flour and fry quickly in boiling oil or fat. Place in a fairly large pan. Cut the onions into rings and braise in the liquid remaining in the frying pan. Remove the pan from the stove, stir in paprika, and pour on 100 ml (4 fl oz) of cold water. Tip the contents of the frying pan over the steaks. Add the crushed clove of garlic and a pinch of caraway seeds. Braise under a lid over low heat until the steaks are nearly done (add water to replace any liquid lost during the cooking). Place the steaks on top of each other and surround them with the sliced green peppers and tomatoes and the peeled, chipped potatoes. Add just sufficient water to cover all the ingredients in the pan, sprinkle with salt, and braise under a lid over low heat until done. (Do not stir—just shake the pan every now and then, taking care not to break up the potatoes). Place the steaks on a hot dish and pile the potatoes on top of them. Sprinkle with the gravy, and decorate with tomatoes, green peppers cut into rings, and parsley. Serve accompanied by pickles.

HAJDÚSÁG PORK SLICES (HAJDÚSÁGI BÖLLÉRPECSENYE)

4 slices of leg of pork (100–150 g—4–6 oz each)
300 g (10 oz) sausage meat containing paprika, suitable for
*   frying*
salt
marjoram
50 g (2 oz) flour
50 ml (2 fl oz) oil for frying
For the garlic sauce:
5–6 fairly large cloves of garlic
30 g (1½ oz) fat or oil
30 g (1½ oz) flour
500 ml (18 fl oz) consommé or meat stock
200 ml (8 fl oz) sour cream
juice of half a lemon
1 tsp sugar
salt
pepper

Beat out the pork slices until thin. Sprinkle lightly with salt and leave to stand for half an hour. Now sprinkle each of them with a pinch of powdered marjoram. Spread the sausage meat evenly over the top of them, roll them up in the form of a cylinder and fasten with skewers or strings. Dip in flour, and fry quickly in hot oil. Now add a little water, and braise, covered, over medium heat until they are done. Leave to cool completely, then cut the meat into not too thin slices. Place in a fire-proof dish. Meanwhile prepare the garlic sauce as follows: lightly brown the flour in the cooking fat. Stir in the crushed garlic (but do not fry it, otherwise it will turn bitter), gradually thin with the meat stock and stir until smooth. Season with salt and pepper and boil thoroughly. Add the sour cream, the sugar, and lemon juice to taste. Bring to the boil once more and pour the sauce over the filled pork slices. Heat them up in a preheated oven and serve with fried potatoes and braised cabbage.
Note: Instead of garlic you may use a finely chopped medium-sized onion, or a large bunch of dill.

BRAISED PORK, BANDIT STYLE (BETYÁRPECSENYE)

4 slices lean leg of pork (150 g—6 oz each)
100 g (4 oz) smoked bacon
1 large onion
250 g (9 oz) champignon or field mushrooms
100 g (4 oz) oil or fat

*150 g (6 oz) **lecsó** (a prepared mixture of cooked green*
*   peppers and tomatoes)*
*   **or** 2 green peppers and 2 tomatoes*
2 cloves of garlic
100 ml (4 fl oz) dry white wine
tarragon
salt
pepper
1 tsp paprika

Beat out the slices of pork a little, a sprinkle with salt, and leave to stand for half an hour. Dice the bacon, fry it, remove the cracklings from the pan, and quickly fry the pork slices in the bacon fat. Set aside. Fry the finely chopped onion until crisp in the liquid remaining in the pan and add the chopped mushrooms. Fry together for a few minutes, then stir in the paprika, the *lecsó* (or the cored green peppers cut into rings and the peeled and quartered tomatoes), and the crushed cloves of garlic. Finally, add the pork slices. Season with salt and pepper, add finely chopped fresh tarragon (or crumbled dried tarragon) to taste, pour the wine into the pan and braise, covered, over low heat until done.
Serve garnished with mixed boiled green vegetables, rice sprinkled with parsley, or potatoes.

KNUCKLE OF PORK, BAKER'S WIFE STYLE (SERTÉSCSÜLÖK PÉKNÉ MÓDRA)

4 medium size, uncooked, knuckles of pork
*   (total weight 1¼–1½ kg–2½–3 ¼ lb including the*
*   bones)*
1 kg (2 lb 3 oz) potatoes
150 g (6 oz) shallots
50 ml (2 fl oz) oil
a bunch of parsley
salt

Carefully wash the knuckles (if there are any bristles remaining on them sear and scrape off).
Sprinkle with salt, leave to stand for about an hour, then wipe dry with a paper napkin. Fry quickly in hot oil over high heat. Now add a little water and braise, covered, over medium heat until nearly done. Remove from the frying pan and place in a baking tin or fire-proof dish. Score the skin all over in a pattern of squares, using a knife with a sharp point. Add the peeled, chipped potatoes and sprinkle a little salt over the top. Bake in a preheated medium oven (180 °C), turning the ingredients over frequently until both knuckles and potatoes are crisp and brown. (Add the shallots when the potatoes are about half done.)
Serve in the baking tin, or arrange the contents on a heated dish, sprinkling chopped parsley over the potatoes on serving. Accompany with salad in season, or pickles.

WAINWRIGHT'S ROAST (STUFFED PORK FLANK) (BOGNÁRPECSENYE—TÖLTÖTT OLDALAS)

800 g (1¾ lb) lean pork thin flank
1 large onion
3–4 cloves of garlic
1 pinch of caraway seeds
100 ml (4 fl oz) dry white wine
For the filling:
150 g (6 oz) minced shoulder of pork
150 g (6 oz) pork liver
1 clove of garlic
1 egg
1 tsp paprika
a pinch of marjoram
salt
pepper

Make a slit in the thin flank, ready for stuffing, sprinkle with salt, and leave to stand for half an hour. Thoroughly mix together the minced meat, the diced liver and the egg. Season with salt, pepper and marjoram to taste, and add the crushed garlic. Use this mixture to stuff the thin flank, firmly stitching up the slit subsequently. Place the meat in a fairly large pan, add the quartered onion, and the cloves of garlic. Sprinkle with the caraway seeds, pour in the wine, and braise, covered, over low heat until half done (replace any liquid lost during the cooking by adding a little water). Now transfer the contents of the pan to a deep baking tin or fire-proof dish. Place it in a preheated oven, and toast at high heat (220° C) for about 25 minutes, basting frequently with its own gravy, until crisp and brown on the outside. Leave it to stand for 10 minutes before serving, otherwise the stuffing may fall to pieces when you start carving.

Fried potatoes, or potatoes cooked with onions, and mixed salad go very well with this dish. It is also excellent cold, but in this case serve a potato and onion salad with it.

POTATO AND ONION SALAD (HAGYMÁS BURGONYASALÁTA)

1 kg (2 lb 3 oz) potatoes (preferably small new ones)
1 large onion
1 large bunch of parsley
50 ml (2 fl oz) salad oil
salt
pepper
1–2 tbsp wine vinegar or lemon juice

Boil the potatoes in their skins, and drain them. Peel while they are still hot, and put them aside to cool. Meanwhile cut the onion into thin slices and sprinkle with a little salt and a tablespoon of vinegar. Cover, and leave for about an hour for the flavours to blend. When the potatoes have cooled, cut them into rounds 3–4 mm (¼ in) thick, add the onion together with its dressing and sprinkle with pepper to taste. Pour in the oil, the chopped parsley and further salt if necessary. Now add the remain-

ing vinegar, and mix loosely together. Keep in the refrigerator, removing it half an hour before serving in case the oil congeals.

This dish is best prepared the day before, but in any case at least 4–5 hours beforehand, to allow the flavours to blend fully.

CABBAGE AND CARROT SALAD (SÁRGARÉPÁS KÁPOSZTASALÁTA)

500 g (1 lb 2 oz) white cabbage
1 medium onion
100 g (4 oz) carrots
1 level tsp ground caraway seed
1 cube of sugar
2–3 tbsp vinegar
2–3 tbsp salad oil
salt

Remove the outer leaves of the cabbage, cut out the stalk, and shred. Take 600 ml (1 pt) of water, add the cube of sugar, the ground caraway seed, and salt and vinegar to taste. Stir well, bring to the boil and simmer for 5 minutes. Meanwhile, clean the carrots and slice with the aid of a cucumber-slicer. Cut the onion into rings, and add both to the shredded cabbage. Pour the boiling hot dressing over the top and mix lightly together. Leave to cool, and keep in the refrigerator until you are ready to serve. Then drain off the liquid, sprinkle a small amount of salad oil over the top, and serve decorated with chopped parsley and slices of tomato.

CURD CHEESE POCKETS (TÚRÓS BUKTA/TÁSKA)

200 g (8 oz) flour
20 g (½ oz) yeast
100 ml (4 fl oz) milk
50 g (2 oz) sugar
salt
a knob of butter the size of a walnut
1 egg yolk for glazing
vanilla flavoured sugar for sprinkling on top
For the filling:
250 g (9 oz) curd cheese (made from cow's milk)
50 g (2 oz) raisins
2 eggs
grated peel of 1 lemon
20 g (½ oz) vanilla flavoured sugar
30–50 g (½ oz) sugar or sweetener to taste

Add the sugar, the crumbled yeast, and 2 tablespoons of flour to the lukewarm milk (i. e. make a ferment). Leave to stand in a slightly warm place for 10–15 minutes. Add the remainder of the flour, and work the dough until it forms blisters. Cover it over with a kitchen cloth, leave it to stand in a warmish place until it doubles its bulk, then roll it out to ½ cm (¼ in) thickness on a floured board. Cut into squares.

While the dough is rising, prepare the filling as follows:

whisk together the curd cheese, the egg yolks, the grated lemon peel and the sugar. Add the previously soaked and drained raisins. Distribute the filling evenly over the squares of dough. Fold the corners over the top and press them gently together. Place in a buttered baking pan. Cover, and set aside again in a warmish place to rise. Brush over with egg yolk, and place in a preheated hot oven (200–220° C) to bake for 35–40 minutes until they are nice and brown.

Sprinkle them with vanilla flavoured sugar on serving.

HONEY MACAROONS (MÉZES PUSZEDLI)

3 eggs
100 g (4 oz) granulated sugar
350 g (13 oz) honey
50 g (2 oz) butter or margarine
700 g (1 lb 10 oz) flour
1 level tsp bicarbonate of soda
a pinch of ground cinnamon
walnuts
hazelnuts

Whisk together the eggs, sugar, honey and margarine. Gradually add the flour, then the bicarbonate of soda, and work well together. Roll the dough out to 3–4 cm (1½ in) thickness on a floured board and cut it into whatever shapes you want (e. g. discs, hearts, stars, crescents etc.). Place a hazelnut or a piece of walnut on top of each, put them side by side on a buttered and floured baking tray, and bake, for a few minutes only, in preheated hot oven (200 °C). (Take great care—they burn very easily, which will give them a bitter taste.)

They will keep for weeks if you put them in an airtight, metal container. In fact, the longer you leave them the nicer, more crispy, they will be.

PASTRY HORN (KÜRTŐSKALÁCS)

For the pastry:
500 g (1 lb 2 oz) fine flour
20 g (½ oz) yeast
2 small cubes of sugar
300–400 ml (½–¾ pt) milk
3 egg yolks and 1 whole egg
50 g (2 oz) melted butter
salt
For the glaze:
2 egg whites
100 g (4 oz) coarsely crushed cubes of sugar
100 g (4 oz) coarsely chopped walnuts or peeled almonds

Traditionally, pastry horns are baked over the embers of an open fire, but they can also be made in an ordinary kitchen oven, as follows: instead of wrapping the strips of dough around a wooden cylinder, wrap them around a rolling-pin about 10–15 cm (4–5 in) diameter, or, for example, a tube-shaped mould. Lay it across the rim of a fairly deep baking tin, so that you can revolve it and continue glazing as you bake.

Add to the flour the egg yolks, the whole egg, the yeast liquefied in 100 ml (4 fl oz) of lukewarm milk sweetened with the cubes of sugar, a pinch of salt, and sufficient lukewarm milk to produce a slightly firmer dough than usual. Add the melted butter and knead until the dough forms blisters. Sprinkle flour over the top, cover, and leave in a warmish place to double its bulk.

Knead gently and roll out on a floured board to the thickness of an inch. Cut into 2–3 cm (½–1 in) strips, and wrap them firmly round the buttered rolling-pin in the form of a spiral, taking care to leave no gaps. Brush each strip with whisked white of egg. Roll them in the mixture of sugar and crushed walnuts, and bake them in the oven (or over not too hot embers), turning them frequently and brushing them with melted butter, until the pastry is golden-brown in colour. Leave it to stand for a few minutes, bang the end of the rolling-pin on the table and slide the pastry horn off it. Sprinkle with vanilla flavoured icing sugar if you wish, and serve while still hot.

Boiled apricot jam thinned down with apricot brandy or *borsodó* (a whisked up wine, sugar and egg sauce similar to egg-nog) are good accompaniments for this pastry.

The recipes were written by Mari Lajos
Design by Vera Köböl
Translated by Dick and Mary Sturgess
Title of the original: Magyarország ízei.
Hortobágy és környéke,
Corvina Kiadó, Budapest, 1990
© Text: Zoltán Halász
© Photographs: Károly Hemző

ISBN 963 13 3023 0
ISSN 0238-7166

Printed in Hungary, 1990
Kossuth Printing House, Budapest